WAVES AND PURTRID

Collection Of Poems

By

CLIFF OYUGI KERAGE

First Edition: September 2019

Published by Lulu Publishers (Lulu.com)

ISBN 978-0-359-92849-1

ACKNOWLEDGEMENT

SPECIAL THANKS TO:

Dr. Christopher Okemwa

APPRECIATIONS TO:

Lewis Wamwanda, Dorothy Nyandega, Angiey Pajero, Dorcas Nabwire

DEDICATED TO:

Caren Jepkogei

Contents

THE PUTRID 5

SCUTTLEBUTT 6

MOTHER 7

FREEDOM DAY 9

TEARS OF A BLACK NATION 11

MR. POLITICIAN 13

XENOPHOBIA 14

I AM A SAVIOUR 15

VOYAGE 17

SWEET MEMORIES 19

TATTERED LOVE 21

DRIP DROP 24

OUT OF ME 25

DAWN 26

BIRD OF JUNO 27

COLOUR OF LOVE 28

LET ME CRY 29

LIMERICK 30

LIMERICK 31
WORDS 32
THOSE WHO 33
VACATION 34
THE UNIVERSE 35
MY MOON 36
WAVES OF LOVE 37
SCARS 38
THIS GIRL 39
BUGSBY 40
CANDY 41
BEAUTEOUS 42
LIFE OF A POET 43
THE BEE 44
PRECIOUS GEM 45
JAWS OF DEATH 46
POSSESED 47
CAGED BIRD 48
SYMPHONY 49
SOIL BAKED EYES 50
WHEN I DIE 51
POWER OF SILENCE 52
BEAUTY OF SIMPLICITY 53
THIS IS NOT POETRY 54
CRUSHING ON A SAPPHIC 55

MY BUTTERFLY 56
SEA OF LOVE 57
I KILLED HIM 58
PICTURE OF MY GIRL 60
BROKEN HEART 61
WHELPED A POOR DEVIL 62
RAIN SOAKED MORNING 66
DORKY 67
CAREN 68
PEACE 69
Hey Ducky 70
LOVE IS A CRAP 71
HOW COULD I EXPLAIN? 72
NIGHT IN THE SAND 73
IF ONLY YOU WERE MINE 74
A MOMENT OF SILENCE PLEASE 75
WAGES OF SIN 78
ME TIME 80
CALL ME A PROSTITUTE 82
LOST SOUL 84

THE PUTRID

Our system riles
This vile system screws
Rapes and defiles
Befouls and infects
With erotically transmitted maladies
Burgles and smuggle like scamp

Our pong system sucks
A crappy structure cankered with scum
Barren to detect no cum
A living carcass gradually decomposing
Going obsolete into abyss of oblivion
With maimed justice oozing pus
A corrupt fascist vitiated in buggery
Piddling depraved scuttlebutt

Our gimpy system a ruin
Debased to shambles by famished wolves
With squalid charismatic paws
Scatters the fruits of our sweat
Squealing it down their cesspool savages
Whose frozen yet rotten hearts
Are corroded with black soot of putrid
Their minds fizzled

Our shitty system a ruin
Exudating venom into lousy blood
Flowing in jigger invested vessels
Our current system reeks like hell
Contaminating the entire society
Crawling and creeping towards purity.

SCUTTLEBUTT

A gazillion of apterous sterile ants follow the path of rules

Shoulders drooping with the weight of levies

They get in through the right ingress looking pallid

No cash to grease the palms at the left

Only to find out that the system has been rigged

Defiled to shambles by winged queen pismires

The Volant ants have politicized everything

Violated it like hungry weevils

After a frenzied few hours of probe

Several high profile arrests are made

To the lame justice oozing pus

The sordid ants are freed on bail

And the lame system flows down the cesspool.

MOTHER

You have broken the vows
Crumbled the cultural heritage
Undressed before the children
And sold your nudity to interlopers

You have gone to bed again
Slept with the aliens like a sporting lady
You have stretched your left hand
With a bowl to the east
And your right hand
Like a pauper to the west

Mother, you have conceived again
So fast like a ruttish rabbit
What is that in your womb
A male child, a messiah
Or, is it war that you are yet to sire?

The frogs are mourning from the seas
The oceans are yearning for abortion
Pleading with you mama
Listen to their woeful cries
Protect the waters from turning red
Trees are quaking with fear

Birds are shivering in their nests
The ancestors are turning with grief in their graves
The wind is carrying a stench of blood
Mother, what is that in your womb?

Your offspring's are weeping from the desert
Torments of the past living in their dreams
Their future looks dark and grubby
Mother, when time is ripe for labor
Never give birth to war again

How about your starved kids
Will you push the nipples of your breasts into their mouths?
Feed them with blood and tears
Or just breastfeed them with milk in peace?

FREEDOM DAY

My heart sinks
And the mind weeps piercingly
Upon seeing people gathered at freedom yard
Singing opus of immunity in jubilation
Proud to be foaled in a den of iniquity
I can read despair and vacation in their eyes
As they sing in praise to the fallen paladins

I can hear umbrageous screams from metropolis
Younkers squalling vociferously from the slums
Pedagogues singing in solidarity for salary increment
Doctors and nurses have dissented too
Patients abandoned to snuff it like insects
Citizenry looking haggard and pallid
Shoulders drooping with the weight of taxation

I can hear a woman and her children shriek in agony
(A husband has committed suicide)
Homicide... Another body dumped in the woods
A young lady executed by her benefactor
Mother crying for justice
People yelling for freedom from paws of wolves

Gunfire deafens my ears
Followed by racking screams and tension
Lachrymator consumes air causing hurly burly
Little school girl lies dead on the road
Two gunshot wounds on her head
Breaking News on my television screen
"Looting criminal gunned down by the police."
Rain of tears falls down my cheeks

I can hear a hungry child cry for food
Several already dead
Vultures feeding on their bony carcasses
I can feel the pain in that old woman mourning in anguish
Her ancestral land has been grabbed by men of great integrity
She has been dispossessed and incapacitated
Man eat man society
With gimpy democracy smelling perfidy
Vitiated to ruination by beguilers
Exoteric funds devoured by grabby savages
Hell has broken loose on freedom day
As we jubilate our independence from exploitation.

TEARS OF A BLACK NATION

It is a dark morning
The birds are too cold to sing
The goddess of war has risen with the sun
Boom! A feeling of tragedy underneath

A black nation is weeping
Tears, fears
Sores, scars
Screams, shuttered dreams
The world is watching with a blind eye
While democracy is being vitiated to shambles
By hungry wolves of impunity
Religion is spitting venom
Creating more animosity
More divisions among the people
Disrupting unity
A sense of humanity is dead
Buried six feet deep in a tomb of pride
Replaced by hostility
Cries of dead souls echoing all over
Bodies of fallen citizens adorning the streets like loaded sacks
Pictures of the injured making headlines

A black nation is at war with its people
Soldiers pointing guns at common citizens
'Dooom d'dooom d'doooom'
Those are not percussion drums
But a storm of bullets flooding the streets
With red pigment
Tires, fire
A cloud of dark smoke
Hellfire blazing across the black land

Communities have risen onto each other's necks

Tears, fears
Swords, spears
And all sorts of crude weapons
Fighting over leadership and religious superiority
The air is breezing screams of sorrow
Wounded voices crying for justice
The world is deaf and dumb
The heaven is giving a taunting stare

A black nation is bleeding
Vegetation painted red
Wet with tears of rue
The wind is carrying a stench of blood
A black society is eating its own race
Survivors are fleeing to deserts and forests
Running for safety and freedom among the wild animals
The freedom gained through struggle and sacrifices

A black nation is seeking for a revolution
To liberate itself from the shackles of despotism
Devolution is never a solution
Rather a synonym of corruption
The people's shoulders are full of blisters
Drooping with the weight of heavy taxation
A black nation is crying for peace and civilization
Who will wipe the tears of a black nation?
If not you and I?

MR. POLITICIAN

I am writing this letter
Under the this scorching sun that is depleting my blood
Trusting that you will read it
Before my skull consumes the last layer of my flesh
I hope I am not asking too much though
Just a drop of water to snuff out the torrid fire in my throat

Mr.Politician
I would have quenched the thirst
With the last drops of my tears
See, there is drought in my eyes
My tears an arid swamp
For three days now,
I have sucked the withered breasts of my mother's carcass lying in dust
Vultures giving me grabby stares
Waiting ravenously for my breath to stop
So they can descend on my bony carcass like a great feast

Mr. Politician
I hope I am not asking too much though
I am aware the roads are impassable
Just a little nutrient to boost my drained energy
Not even worth the ballot boxes you brought
Let alone the dams and boreholes you promised
Just a drop of water to keep my heart beating
My voice speaking for the voiceless
Before hyenas scatter my skeletons.

XENOPHOBIA

Black is sacred
Zulu or Igbo
Blood is all red
We are one people
Why all this hatred?

Tears, fears
Swords, spears
War, bloodshed
Humanity is dead
Tires, fire
Right and left
No shred of tenderness left
Society devouring its own race
All because of vanity

A black nation is bleeding
Screams of pain
Dreams full of stain
Africa is weeping
Where did we go wrong?
The freedom we fought for so long
The heritage we defended so strong
Is here to eat us
We have lost a sense of belonging
And buried it deep in the grave of pride
Our mother land is falling apart
All because of ignorance and greed
When will we wake up to civilization?
See us as one people
Speaking a common language of humanity?

I AM A SAVIOUR

Call it blasphemy,
or judge me with treason
Maybe I have lost some sense of reason
but I am sorry to say;
I am a savior
A messiah
fully charged with a great desire
to save people from the aura of affliction

I worship the unseen God
The Mind, who existed before creation
maker of all civilization
eye of the blind that sees beyond imagination
creator of the idea behind the universe
the word that flows in verse
nothing can be compared to you my lord
the computers have tried but not beyond your reason

Just like Jesus is said to have a mission
to save humanity from sin and oppression
I also have a great mission and vision on earth
to save crushed souls from the chains of pain and depression
through poesy, my religion
I breathe new life to broken hearts
and light sparkles of hope to gloomy souls

I am a voice that speaks for the voiceless
as I flow with divine healing
spit the fire that consumes demons
cut through like a sword back and forth
with the gospel of truth and justice
that can turn happiness to sorrow
and wipe out tears of rue in darkness'
I break the walls of emotional prison
set free the detained soul
'I am who I am'
I am the word that flows in verse
I am POETRY.

VOYAGE

Like a solitary wayfarer on voyage
I have traveled on briary mountains of pain
Roved through deserted swamps of dejection
Sailed against the tides in stormy seas of sorrow
Swirled by emotional whirlwind in the isle fate

I have seen mornings blossom like roses
evenings wither like autumn leaves
I have watched the sun fall beyond the skyline
dark days reign the aura

I have heard a cacophony of cricket chirrups
Suicide thoughts battling in my mind
The moon peeking at me like a spy
Lost my myself into a series of emotional detention
Seen my dreams of better days turn into nightmares

I have seen grey wool form in my eyelids
Heavy rains fall down my cheeks
Felt my world torn apart
Draining my future dreams and aspirations
While the heavens giving me a taunting stare

My key to success has drowned in a pool of tears
The world around me has scorned me like an alien
I have beared the heavy weight of my swollen heart
Swallowed the bitter herb of truth
Tasted the sweetness of betrayal
Each time my shadow walks out of me
Leaving me dumped in the ruins
I have been buried each moment a piece of me dies deep inside

I have searched through my soul
Looked deep into memories of my past

Found my childhood self-hiding deep within
He has been leading my soul into wounds
Yet still he cries for attention like a little baby

I have woken to reality that life is a flowing river
So full of hungry crocodiles
And I am a wildebeest waiting anxiously at the verge
To cross to the other side where pastures are greener.

SWEET MEMORIES

I try to fake a smile
Pretend that everything is fine
The truth hits me hard like chime
Memories of you keep repeating identically
Tormenting me every night
I have lost every bit of me
Deep within i am an empty shell
So light like a chick's feather

Since the day your shadow walked out of me
Life has become vapid
Completely insignificant
I try to seek solace in the bottle
To soothe my broken heart

I look myself in the mirror
An image of you appears again
I turn fast and sit on the edge of my bed
Loneliness patting me gently on my shoulder
I look at your picture
The memories of you flashback in my mind
I remember how we sat
On my bed facing each other
Squeezing chips into each other's mouths
Chortling like little babies
Then you held me tight
Close to your erect knockers
We sank ourselves into my sheets and sinned

You wanted more and more till dawn
(As if for the last time)
I sublimed into your soul
How I wish time could revive itself
And the dreams of better days become real
How I yearn for those golden old days of eros and roses
Before my heart snows.

TATTERED LOVE

There is drought in my eyes
My tears are dry like an arid swamp
I am not crying though
It is just that.... sometimes droplets ooze from my soul
and wet my eyelids

I am a common African woman
With withered breasts drooping with the weight of a newborn
No more milk left in them
My body wrinkled and worn out
Not because I am ageing
But due to dark emotional memories
The skull inside me rages with fury
As I rove about in this desert of sorrow
Where you dumped me
With a seed of you sprouting in my womb
Almost naked
In tattered bloomers

I am a maimed skylark
Singing a lullaby song
While nursing my emotional wounds
The pain inflicted in my heart lives on

I still remember
How you plucked me like a bloom
From my mother's cartilage
I was a bud
Beautiful like Eden's daisies
We bowed before my father's grave and took a vow
To love and cherish each other
(Till death sunders us apart)

You carried me on your shoulders

Gave me shelter in your heart
That gave me a sigh of relief
Each night lit sparkles of bliss in my heart
The caresses and kisses
The warmth of your tight embrace
All made me feel complete like a full moon

We made love each night
Chuckled amid cricket sounds
Swished like sea breeze
You sowed a seed in me
Then the goddess of war awoke
The sun set upon me
Midnight silence barked furiously
The clouds darkened
The floods washed away
The vows we made
The dreams we shared
Love and everything else

A demon replaced your soul
Turning you into a hideous beast
Our bed became a battlefield of swords
And everything that was within your reach
I became a drum for you to hit hard
It became a routine
The sheets became wet
Not with orgasm but red pigment

I was served with blows along my breakfast
Some spilled on my tummy
I ate my woeful tears for lunch
My face adorned with scar sores

You called me a whore
A helpless bloody witch
Threw me out of your life
I forgive you.... You didn't know
But can't you at least hear the cries of your flesh
Screaming all through the night
Amid caresses and lullaby songs
Can't you listen to the weeping voice of your blood?
The seed that you planted and vanished like fog?

DRIP DROP

I am seated solitary by the window

The sun goes down fading like fog

Grey sheep walks tardily in the sky

Drip drop, drop drip drizzling mizzle

Trees dancing to the swishing whistle

Cricket chirps, bird chirrups twitter in the air

Drip drop, drop drip drizzling mizzle

Rub-a-dub, rub-a-dub goes my chest

I peep through a hole on my door knob

The moon peeks at me like a secret agent

Drip drop, drop drip drizzling mizzle

Squeaks and shrieks fill the air as darkness withers.

OUT OF ME

I just want to walk out of me

Run fast past myself and leave this life behind

Go down with the falling sun

Never to show up again at dawn

I don't want to see the face of this world

All I need is a little toxicant

Just to soothe my sleep tonight

A bottle of pills and whiskey will do me fine

I yearn to wake up in a different world

Where my wretched old life does not exist

And my emotions will never explode.

DAWN

Gloomy days will wither like autumn leaves
The night will vanish into oblivion
My demons will drop dead and lapse
Darkness will fade away like heated mist
The moon will hide behind the sheep
Chirps of birds and insects will fill the air
Followed by gentle hums of the wind
Grey wool will form in my eyes
A drizzle of bliss fall down my cheeks

The rain of roses and herbs will pour
Wash away my stain of pain
My scars sores will heal
There will be drought in my eyes
The whirlwind tide will tranquilize in my soul
The emotional storm will calm down and fog fleet

Then I will sail through like a ship
On the sea of love and peace
Fly high into the sky like the bird of Jove
And shine bright to the world like Day star.

BIRD OF JUNO

The sun sinks quietly into slumber
Dusk rises to reign the aura
Cricket chirrups fill the air
A face peeks from the rear of my door
Like the moon beyond the woolen sky
A peafowl moves towards me
Eyes flickering like fireflies

She spreads her wings like a skylark
Swirls my emotions like whirlwind
Tides my heart in a storm of love
The night goes silent like a tomb
Everything seems to be stone dead
Sighs and chirrups breeze the air
Squeaks and shrieks dwindle the ambiance
Faint chirps are muttered in silence

I open my eyes at dawn
To witness the sun peeking alluringly
Tepid like sun rays in a mizzle
The birds are praising outside
The wind is whistling swimmingly
The legions are murmuring stealthily
Amid caresses and kisses with bird of Juno.

COLOUR OF LOVE

What is the color of love?
Is it red like ripe cherries?
Or blue like the sky above
That soothe my dark soul
When I am feeling blue?

White they said is for peace
When they came like butterflies from the seas
With Bibles in their hands
And weapons in their pockets
Black is evil they made me believe
The angels are while and of course felice
The devil is black our common belief

Our fathers were so green
When they accepted the colorless lies
That red is the color of war
But valentines faces become grin
With red roses, red kisses and red clad

What is the color of love?
Is it red like the blood of war?
Or yellow-green like olive?

LET ME CRY

Let me shed my tears
Sob out my layers of disguise
Free myself from my demons

Let me cry all my heart out
Release a valium of teardrops into my aching soul
Cry out the pain of my scar sores

Let each driblet speak out loud
And tell a tale of my darkest memories
Let me yell out my sea of sorrow
My eyes overflow with a lake of tears
For the world to see my emotional wounds

Let me cry myself out
Wash out my stain of pain
Let grey clouds form in my eyelids
Salty rain flow down my cheeks
I want to swim in my ocean of tears
And cool down the raging devils burning up in me.

LIMERICK

There once live a girl named Maggie

Whose knockers were erect and baggie

She was slender and tall

Loved and admired by all

Though her dressing funny and hair shaggy

LIMERICK

There once live a sense of humanity

When people were free from insanity

Hearts were full of love

People treated without glove

A time when conscience valued divinity

WORDS

I wish I were words
So you feel me each moment you write
Or maybe, if I were a lollipop
You'd kiss me each time you suck.

THOSE WHO

Those who don't read
Those who don't write
Are like plants
They have no conscience
They have no sense of humor

Those who don't read
Those who don't write
Are like plants
They are living
Yet they have no feelings.

VACATION

Meet me at the Indian ocean
Let us listen to the waves' percussion
As the breeze whistles a sweet symphony
Let our hearts dance to the rhythm of the sea
As it rises and falls ashore

Let me open a new page in your heart
Write you a sweet song of love
Palm leaves dance to the chorus in jubilation
Birds chirrup a lyrical euphony in unison

Let me squeeze you on my hard chest
Rub myself gently on your erect knockers
Fall deep into the sea of love and rest
As I feel the fragrance of your scented breath

Let me sink into your rose petals
And suck the cloying pollen bliss
As I narrate to you the amorous tale
A tale of how hearts mated in twilight.

THE UNIVERSE

Gazing into the universe in your eyes
My mind fades in a daze
The moon that hides in them
Sets my emotions ablaze

Sometimes they gleam like blue flames
Putting twinkling diamonds to shame
The stars in your eyes make me shy
With their bright light like the sun in the sky
They embellish like rainbow when you cry

When they stare at me like rising dawn
They have magic that heals my pain
Each moment I see your charismatic eyes
I always want to drown in their ice
And warm myself in the fire hiding in their iris.

MY MOON

Like a waning moon in gloomy glam
Your eyes are serene like rising dawn
Drawing my emotions like charisma
Your pulchritudinous face waxing gibbous
Your bright smiles fades my pain in a daze

You are the star above the Indian Ocean
My symphonic songbird in the morning
The nightingale in twilight
The lullaby in my night dreams
Whose mellifluous melody soothes me to sleep?

Your splendid figure like the wasp
When you walk my soul trips the light fantastic
My heart grimaces upon seeing your squashy skin like silk
The mouth covets for your red lips
How am I supposed to let you know?
You are my rosemary
Your fragrant breath a soul herb

I crush on your picturesque photos
And sin in my drawers every night
Your coiffure drives me gaga
As it lies stunningly on your face.

WAVES OF LOVE

Love is an ocean
So full of emotional waves
Flowing on like The Nile

Sometimes it storms like a tsunami
Tides my soul back and forth
I try swimming fast to the shores
Its whirlwind swirls me deep
Drowning me into its depths realms

Sometimes it calms like a pool
Sending its cool breeze ashore
I dive into its still water
When my blood is blazing hot
And chills my emotions to stillness

I lie in the salty sand by the shore
Watching the moon waxing gibbous
When the ocean is not good for sailing through
I see a reflection of stars beaming
As it breezes a sweet symphony
The wave's percussion rises and falls
My heart dances to the lyrical
Of the ocean blue of love.

SCARS

Tears, fears

Stain, pain

Piercing my heart like a spear

My death seems so near

My breath about to disappear

Sores, scars

Dreams, screams

Fire in my swelling throat

My raging skull forcing its way out

My soul is numb but I am feeling ouch!

You asked if I am crying.

No, it is just that raindrops ooze from deep within

And wet my eyelids

Never mind

I am just fine.

THIS GIRL

This girl is a professed thief
For she broke into my soul
Stole my heart at first sight

She must have been moulded with fine clay
Extracted from the sun
For the way she is hot
Sets my emotions on fire
This girl is mean
She can't give me peace of mind
The only thing she offers is sleepless nights

I would say she is a witch
For she has possessed my feelings like a demon
Drowned me deep in the ocean of love
I can't even retrieve myself

Her eyes are bewitching
The sparkles in them draw me like charisma
Perverting my mind with her juju smiles
Turning me to a romantic zombie

This girl is my moon
Her face lightens my dark soul
The ocean blue in her eyes reflects stars
That put twinkling diamonds to shame
Her soft skin is my sweet banana
So yummy like drinking chocolate

Her love is like concentrated alcohol
Just a drop of it throws me out of control
Makes me feel weak and high
She is narcotic like bhang
Each moment with her leads to addiction
I can't resist her force of attraction
I have lost myself into this girl.

BUGSBY

My precious little bunny
So chummy and always funny
I can't believe you are gone honey
Leaving me in this cold
Watching you in dismay

My eyes are soaked in salty rain
My heart is weeping in silence
As I gently caress your sleek fur
Wishing I could give you my breath
And bring you to life little pet

My house now looks empty
Full of darkness without your cunning eyes
So ugly without your stunning moves
I will always miss you runty rabbit
May your teansy soul rest in peace.

CANDY

Sweet candy dishy and simple
Soft face like doll with no pimple
Giggles embellish chubby cheeks with dimples

Eyes scintillate like diamonds
Charismatic lips red like cherry
Comely hair curl like jasmine

Voice gentle and sweet like a coo
My oscine bird when I am feeling blue
Her breath ocean breeze in sweltering days
Eyes like sunrays in drizzling mizzle

My symphony is solitary nights
A soothing berceuse in my dreams
Bird of Jove, the one I truly love.

BEAUTEOUS

A beauteous butterfly is she
Her wings like sunflower all can see
Blue eyes like sky above the sea

Her gyre hair sprucely kinked like festoon
Dinky face Sheeny like noon
Voice sweet like bassoon
Always charming and funny like cartoon

My heart goes pit-a-pat with her warm smile
I see blues watching her walking style
As she saunters tardily down the isle
Emotions flow in my spine like The Nile.

LIFE OF A POET

I write out my mind
Share feelings to the blind
Who read it and get touched
With poignant flow of emotions
They say my poetry is awesome
"Gosh !"
"Cliff you are handsome."

I fake a smile on my face
My eyes never smile back
I laugh to gratify my friends
Yet my heart is soaked in tears
At the bottom of my bosom
Lies a real Cliff
An ugly me
A worn out me
A broken and crushed me
Shackled in emotional detention
Chained in darkness to a web of pain

Deep within my soul
A bully assaults me daily
He rapes and defiles my innocence
Kills a piece of me in silence
He haunts me in my dreams
Warns to give me no peace
He hands me an incisive knife
And orders me to take my life

People do celebrate me
And say my poetry inspires
Others yearn to see me
My appearance they admire
I wish they could see beyond my dark skin
Look at me deep within
And realize how much I have expired.

THE BEE

New dawn peeps from beyond
The air is filled with canorous chirps
The wind is humming gently in praise
Trees dancing in jubilation
I look out through the window
It is a beautiful day

I see a buzzing bee
Flaring happily in the morning dew
I watch keenly
It settles on a thorny leaf
Soothing itself in sunshine warmth
The cool breeze caresses it gently
A butterfly intrudes
Disturbing its peace

Buzz buzz buzz
Away towards the rosebush
The amazing sensation of sweet scent
Mesmerizes its little soul

I see it flying swiftly
From flower to flower
As it sings
A song of love
It spots a scenic yellow rose
Lands on its petal like a plane
Whispers to it, a song of love
It kisses the bloom's bud deeply
And buzzes in bliss back to the hive.

PRECIOUS GEM

I wonder why the buzzing bees
Have not smelt this scented rose
Blooming and glistening among the violets

Everything about it ignites a spark
It is the colours in the rainbow
Its petals the moon that lights the night
Velvety and soft like silk
Makes its rosebud shine like diamonds

Her breath is the ocean breeze
Emitting sweet fragrance that soothes the nose
Its silk leaves sweet like chocolate
A beautiful angelic African queen
The precious gem and jewel
Whose picture puts angels to shame?
My soul dances to the lyrical tunes of her bud
Each time I set my eyes on her
Her face melts my heart
I always yearn to bask in her warm smiles.

JAWS OF DEATH

At the verge of a cliff
I stood solitary and static
A rain of tears falling down my soppy cheeks
My face was blanketed by darkness in daylight
The world seemed dead to me
I felt devoid and utterly lost
Deep within I was numb frozen
Yet my emotions were boiling deep

Demons were battling in my raging skull
My soul crushed into ashes
The walls of my heart were collapsing
Pain pierced through my emotional wounds
Ripping my scar sores apart
All I wanted was to end this war
Kill the emotional pain
All I wanted was to listen to my devils

I felt hollow like an empty shell
Nothing else left inside me
I wanted to fall right into hell
Burn my affliction to ashes
Voices of skeletons echoed in my mind
Calling me to the land of peace and solitude
But then, I decided to face my raging devils
Battle with them one final time.

POSSESED

He is here again
My demon
Glaring at me
Haunting my mind
My blood is boiling
Body soaked in sweat
Hands are quaking
Feeling hot
I can't resist the fire
Phallus almost bursting
Alone
Locked in my room
Naked
I sink in my sheets
Hand on it
Sinning
Sighs filling the ambiance
My devils cooling down
Shrinks
Relieved
Allayed
Goes back to sleep
Leaving me lying
Whacked
Feeling empty
A wrecking difference.

CAGED BIRD

A maimed bird locked in a cage
Flipping her little flimsy wings
Chirping chirrups full of rage
Leashed to despair as she flings
Resigned, she lies in the cage
Opus of immunity now she sings

The caged bird has no choice
No other way to assuage her throbbing pain
But to let it out through her wounded voice
She sobs and sings again and again
Clings to her fading hope of rejoice
Hopping her freedom she will soon gain.

SYMPHONY

Sweet little songbird
Would you be the symphony?
That soothes my frail heart
When I am feeling so low?

Would you spread your wings?
Like the bird of Jove
Sing me a song of love,
Protect me like a hopeless dove
Liberated from a hawks jaw?

Would you hold my hand tight?
Walk me across the shore
Dance with me in the moonlight
And play along with me like a baby doll?

Be my rose for a moment
Make me your buzzing bee in the morning dew
Be my juicy bloom that withers not
My cute little oscine bird
Would you be my symphony in twilight?

SOIL BAKED EYES

Those mild brown eyes
So cool like muddy ice
The lake of brown
In its depths I drown
As golden beam they shine
Like a glass of vintage wine

Those sun dazed eyes
Warm like drinking chocolate
So sweet like flavored honey
A mixture of day and night
An occultation they create
Benignity flows in their lake
They are sun baked soil
Just like morning coffee
My emotions they boil.

WHEN I DIE

My time will come when breath will bid goodbye
My heart will snow and I will finally die
Do not stand near my grave and cry
I will fade like smoke into clouds in the sky
I know it will hurt but just try
Tell the world I tried but life I couldn't buy

Let people know I suffered so long
When my spirit responds to the gong
My soul will fly to where I belong
Do not weep for me, just be strong
Never even wish to come along

I will be happy when I am gone
Free from pain and never alone
With my ancestors in the underworld zone
Do not wear a face of grief and groan
Into the land of solitude I will be blown
In a different world I will be born.

POWER OF SILENCE

I opt to detain my words in a cage
Just to preserve my running breathe
And lull my slushy emotions of rage

I sink myself in the depth realms of muteness
Drown my thoughts in an ocean of wisdom
As I listen to the sound waves of quietness

My voice of silence is visible to the eyes
As it rains down my soppy cheeks
Beauty of tranquil shines in my smiles like galaxy
Calming my emotional whirlwind to stillness

My mind gets lost in a forest of forlornness
The atmosphere becomes a mirror
I stare into it and see nothing but myself

My thoughts speaking so loud
They scream enough to break a glass
But on the outside I don't utter

The colorful sound of quietude says it all
There is comfort in silence
Calming emotional storm to hush

BEAUTY OF SIMPLICITY

Do you ever think of every morning?
How it chirps in praise
Sweet melodies like jazz
As early
No alarm
No home
Just nothingness?
But then with humility
It finds a branch to settle on
With self-motivation it builds a nest
Sinewy for heavy whirlwind and rainstorm
Simple and cozy than crowded slums
With hope it spreads its wings
And searches for food
No farm
No harvest
No promised future
But then it trusts and lives on desire

I watch it moving swiftly in the air
Higher into the clouds like a lark
Chirping and dancing to its lyrical chirrups
Not minding about tomorrow
Knows no pain or sorrow
Its flamboyant feathers
So comely and dinky
Beauty of purity within simplicity

THIS IS NOT POETRY

But words oozing right from my soul
Come on, don't look at me in that tone of voice
When I spit it out that you are my choice
The one I will treat like a joke
When I carry you around the house each night
As we play hide and seeking in the sheets
While chuckling like little babies

This is not poetry
I will wipe out your tears
Kiss your emotional wounds
Or even lick your scars
I will sing you poetry songs
Soothe you to sleep in my arms
I will make the symphony sweeter
And keep your dreams longer

When you are fire I will be water
I will carry your pain on my shoulder
Shed your tears in the bathroom
I bet you will lose trace to the kitchen
For I will always cook your food
Serve it to you while still warm
You got to trust me darling
This is not POETRY

CRUSHING ON A SAPPHIC

I saw them kissing
Thought they were teasing
Like self-pollinating roses
Lips percussion in the air
Tongues interlocked
Eyes closed

They were hissing
Like mating snakes
My heart crashed
For there was my crush
I swallowed saliva and coveted in tears

She unlaced the blue blouse
Of my all-time crush
I saw them peeping
Like two ripe mangoes
She sucked them gently
As my crush danced
To the rhythm of her lips
I couldn't help teardrops
Rolling down my cheeks
I wished to scream loud
To scatter the heavens
But helplessly with Eros
I watched them sinning
My steamy puppy swinging
And barking furiously.

MY BUTTERFLY

Alone and dejected I sat
Watching the sun make one last blink
Before she sank beyond the skyline
Billowy clouds like a gazillion of sheep grazing in the sky
Gusty wind massaged my warm cheeks like ocean breeze
A braw butterfly emerged from foggy haze
Fluttering her golden fragile wings

I gazed at her lustfully as she kissed the rose petals
My mind envisaged as she flipped towards me
Soul danced to the pit-a-pat of in my chest
I felt her tender wings caress my cheeks gently
She opened her colorful wings and fluttered away
I smelt the sweet scent of her shadow
Wished to fly along with her to the forest of roses
And dance to the rhythm of her wings as she swings

SEA OF LOVE

I drown in your sea of love
To dwell in the surface of your heart
Where tides of bliss are cool like morning dew
The waves massaging my body all through
As they whisper rhythmic melodies to me
While rub-a-dub of your heart echoes in my ears

I want to bath in the ocean blue of your love
Wash out my tears of rue and pain
To the shores of warm breeze I will swim
To warm myself in the sunshine sparkles of your smiles
As my soul dances to your symphonic song of love
And the fragrant breeze fill my heart with joy.

I KILLED HIM

I have a confession to make
Yes, I am guilty
I killed him
He died for my sake
Up on the cross at Calvary
He cried in pain for my sins
I laughed and mocked the king of kings
Scorned and sneered as I nailed his hands
Speared him as I jeered with pride

I abused his power and worth
Accused him for my affliction
Adorned his head with thorns
Yet still he was willing to cleanse my soul
With his precious blood

He looked down at me with loving eyes
Gave me a tender smile
Then he raised his breath to the heavens and cried
"Father, forgive him for he knows not what he is doing."
I watched his last drop of blood
He looked at me and said,
"It is finished."

He forgave all my sins
I stood there static
Hands soaked in blood
Heart swelling with regret
I came to myself way too late
I had killed an innocent man
He was right there on the cross
The Messiah

Tortured to death
It dawned on me that I needed a savior
He was buried in a tomb
On the third day he defeated death and resurrected
He went to his father, to prepare a place for me
He lives.

PICTURE OF MY GIRL

Painting a picture of my girl
detained in a prison of depression
her face soaked in the sea waves of dark memories
her eyes sunken and closed
tears of rue dripping down her soppy cheeks
her wrist adorned with bruises from razor cuts
she is holding a bottle of whiskey in her frozen hands
looking perturbed and dejected
soul scattered,
trust shattered,
innocence murdered

She is drowned in so much fright
Identical images of the pain she felt that night
keeps flashing back in her mind
how he pinned her against the rough wall
tied her hair to a snag
like a maimed caged bird
she tried to fly away
her wings had been broken

He killed her soul several times
as he rolled his sword deeper
cutting through the walls of her rosebud
the moon watched with pity
as he butchered her pride
mashed her heart into pieces
deflowered her dignity
vitiated her treasure
left her scattered
oozing blood filled with his filth
my paper is soaked in tears
my pencil is sobbing in silence
as I draw this picture of my girl
the girl I so much love
but she hates herself and everything in sight

BROKEN HEART

You see this frail heart of mine
I lay it bare in your hands
Hold it with care and tenderness
Never let it slip off your fingers

It has endured so much pain
It has been fallen and broken several times
Faced total rejection
Suffered too much dejection
It has been torn into shreds
Its trust shattered
Innocence defiled and murdered

Never let it fall apart again
It has taken me ages
To collect its crushed pieces
Sew it back to wholeness
See, it is full of loose stitches
Emotional scars of betrayal

It is wet with tears of rue
Keep it warm in your soul
Never expose it to too much heat
It might explode to ashes
Just treat it like a treasure
And not a playground for leisure.

WHELPED A POOR DEVIL

You scorn me for no good reason
I am human too with emotions like you
well, don't look at me in that tone of voice
regarding me as an object
put to existence for the same reason as liquor
you just need to infer the fact that,
I had no choice
otherwise I would have wished not to be born

yes I am a cull
Secernated like an alien
a desolate lone wolf
with tears leaking into wounds
a piece of me dying inside

Go on,
cogitate
spite and skewer venom on me
squelch my soul
rip my emotional scars apart
with all sorts of revilement
call me a whoreson
a mongrel
or rather a bastard
Because that is what I am
Yes I am a son of a bitch
I wish the world would just understand
that it is not my fault
and entirely blame the feckless felon
who viciously vitiated and defiled
a vernal virtuous girl and vanished

I am a discarded puppy
Nerve-wracking in a bitch womb
whelped to relish gustatory sensation of distress
dispossessed like a vagrant

In this ragged macrocosm torn apart
the sun scorching like an inferno
draining my soul into shrivel
my soul submerged in phony illusion
hunting the nefarious dog of impunity
who planted a seed and vaporized.
Our Father
who art in heaven
you said that,
you created me in your own image
and I looked myself in the mirror
couldn't see any likeness of you
but a crushed soul
created in the image of pain
forsaken to languish in distress
tears of rue leaking into bleeding sores
oh God, you lied to me this is not fair

You told me that,
all are equal before your eyes and I trusted you
Yet last night.... Last night
I slept on an empty stomach
with a mocking aroma from my neighbor's kitchen
I kept calling on your name and ended up feeding on my woeful tears
as if that was not enough
today.... just today
a dear friend died right before me
as I shouted a healing intercession
Oh God you disappointed me this is not fair

Your silence is wrecking me
tearing me into pieces
as you watch with a blind eye
acting deaf and dumb
as if you ain't there
I am your own image remember
why do I have to suffer in your likeness

how long will I shed tears to gain your attention
Yet still I keep trusting you?

You said that,
I should ask and I will be given
knock and it shall be opened
but my doors are locked tight no matter how I try
I have always asked for bliss and sorrow is all I receive

"Blessed are those who mourn for they shall be comforted"
my story seems opposite
for I am cursed no matter how I cry

What hurts me most is the itching fact that,
murderers, thieves, corrupt masters
and all sorts of evil people
are swimming in a pool of blessings
while I am left alone
to swim against the tides in torrents of tears
My shoulders are full of blisters
I am tired of carrying this heavy yoke of burdens
That is drowning me in an ocean of sorrow
with faded hopes for a better tomorrow
I am a laughing stock
see, my knees are full of scars
my eyes bleeding agony of shame
Lord of mercy
you have betrayed my trust

where are you hiding your face
I just feel like a snake eating its own tail
I am like a child
who wants to cross to the other side but there is a deep ditch

I try to stop thinking
but can't find the heart and courage to
I still fear you God
I keep calling on you

with the last drops of energy left
I keep trusting you with my faith
as little as a mustard seed
my hopes and aspirations hanging on your thumb
as I seek first your kingdom
and all shall be added unto me
I believe and trust that one day
you will have it in your heart
to remember that I am your likeness
created in your own image

RAIN SOAKED MORNING

This rain soaked morning
Trees were mourning above the meadow
Forest of rain beyond my window
Dripping background was felt deep
As the day slipped away into the rain

DORKY

Do you hear that bird,
On the tallest palm tree,
Raising and falling its tone?
Kisses of love it chirrups
Your message from me it brings.

CAREN

Can you sing me
A sweet symphony
Right in this dim twilight
Embrace me a little more
Never to let me fall out of love?

PEACE

People of Gusii were bounded by enyamumbo
Enyamumbo our cultural heritage
A common belief that strengthened our bond
Cultural norms that cemented our unity
Each clan existed in harmony pouring libation to Chisokoro (ancestors).

Hey Ducky

I wanted to save your picture in my gallery
Just in case you decided to hide your face
I wanted to save it on the shelves of my mind
Just in case I lost my sight
But then,
I remembered to pin it on the walls of my heart
Just in case I lost my memory
And glued it all over my soul
Just in case I lost my breath.

LOVE IS A CRAP

Who said love is blind?
Well, he was absolutely right
Maybe I have lost my sight

How I wish it is just a dream
For I have become a total fool
I feel like I should scream
Before I drown into this pool

I met this beautiful girl named Joy
Short and dark like a blackberry
With a seamless skin like a toy
Fragrance sweet like a rosemary

Her sunbaked eyes so charming
Drowning my mind into a daze
Her warm smiles are bewitching
Setting my emotions ablaze

I fell deeply in the ocean of love
She turned down my proposal
I promised her the moon and stars above
She scorned my face with a disposal

Why can't I rest at night?
Counting the stars in the sky
People ask if I am alright
All I do is look into space and cry

Why can't I just understand?
The fact that she loves her boyfriend
The one she calls a future husband
And I can be only a friend?

HOW COULD I EXPLAIN?

Seated on a coach
Playing with my little baby
Feeling her little tender touch
Her name is Princess Daisy

My wife had left carrying her purple pouch
For a meeting at the church maybe
Then came swabbing the floor, body in crouch
Our housemaid, a beautiful young lady

The picture of her transparent dress
Lost my mind in a daze
She threw me into a total mess
Boiling my blood, setting emotions ablaze

The cry of baby Daisy became meaningless
Everything in the house turned into haze
I was tempted to caress and undress
I couldn't help but just gaze

Eyes popped out like a light bulb
My trousers ticking like a clock
I imagined myself in a nightclub
Dancing with her, souls interlock
My mind was still in the pub
When my wife entered without a knock
Her eyes on my wet trousers as I tried to rub.

NIGHT IN THE SAND

A night when crickets were too cold to chirp
Chirp in praise to the waning moon
Moon illuminated the night in blues
Blues reflected in the Indian Ocean
Ocean where I lay in the sand by the shore
Shore where she sat beside me leaning against the wind
Wind whistled as we were drinking
Drinking from a bowl full of cool breeze
Breeze that kissed our skins gently
Gently as we happily scanned the heavens so star filled
Filled with our love bounded in the blue sky above
Above the rhythmical waves where we were blanketed
Blanketed by the salty oceanic water.

IF ONLY YOU WERE MINE

I would wake to your face like rising dawn
To smell the fragrance of your rose petals
Look straight into your sunbaked eyes
So cool like a glass of vintage wine
Bask in your warm smiles like sunshine

If only you were mine
I would fall deep into your heart
Drown into your sea of love
Let you dwell in the depth realms of my soul
Away from the whirlwind storm and heavy rains
I would protect you from sorrow and pain

If only you were mine
I would spread my wings like a lark
Hold you tight and show you how to fly
Take you for honeymoon in the sky
And ask the moon to sing you a lullaby
The stars would dance like butterflies
Deep in your velvety petals I would be
To suck the sweet pollen like the buzzing bee
If only you were mine.

A MOMENT OF SILENCE PLEASE

It is now a week since I was buried
my spirit is still mourning
my own death that came hitting without warning
If tears could speak
mine could have a story to tell about my demise

That fateful night,
The moon was shining so bright
I came home late
Just to face my bitter reality of fate
I knew any moment I could lose my breath
because the doctors had predicted my death
advised me to write a will
or make short term plans at will
I had battled with chronic cancer for so long
Though I had taught myself to be strong

But that night... That night I met my worst
she must have been carried by a storm of emotional waves
drowning herself in the depth realms of Eros
and forgot to lock the main door
so I walked up the corridor
stood right at my bedroom door
ready to strike her with a surprise
little did I know that she too got me a big surprise

I was about to knock
when a strange sound struck my ear
awakening my storm of fear
I peeped through a hole on my door knob
what met my eyes sent me to sob
I couldn't believe my lovely wife
on top of him, sharing honey from my hive
right on our matrimonial bed
my demons pushed me to render someone dead

I rushed to the kitchen and grabbed a knife
flung the door open ready to take a life
I was about to stab his chest deep
when he grabbed my neck like a whip
squeezed it hard, sending me to a sound sleep
I never woke up to fight back or say goodbye
that's how I died

A few days later
The postmortem reports indicated I died of cancer
How I wish my tears could speak and testify
I get myself buried six feet deep each night
whenever I see my wife sinning with him
on our favorite sheets
her sighs and screams of felicity never let me rest in peace
as I witness and mourn my own dead in silence
I died in pain
and I am resting in vain.

WAGES OF SIN

You call it guilt?
Well, mine is beyond darkness of doom
I want to confess
But the lump in my throat chocks me up

The very night of my friend's death
Tragedy struck
I got lost of my control
An irresistible desire set my emotions ablaze
Boiled up my blood
With an urge to quench my burning throat

I sinned with her husband
Under their favorite bed sheets
I lost my innocence
To the very matrimonial be that swallowed my pride
Now I remain a prisoner to my actions
With my conscience cuffed
Self-confidence chained
I look myself in the mirror
All I see is trash
Engulfed in wishes of having tables turned
For the tides of regret are drowning me dead
I am lost in a gloomy forest of hopes
Of what I couldn't have done

She didn't rest in peace
Her spirit shattered in pieces
I know she cried to the grave
And the taught of it
Sends me to an abyss of suicidal thoughts
Wishing it was me

I want to commit my last mistake
pay my wages of sin
A blade through my veins

So I breathe my last breath
I want my apology to reach her in person
So I am sure she will forgive me
I am doing this to correct my mistakes
Paying with life for the betrayal I caused
Too bad he made the mistake to appear too good
My hunger then can't justify my actions now
I feel like I am a reincarnation of evil
It is my last pulse
Ultimate sacrifice
Final breath
Perfect goodbye
I have confessed on earth
And I depart to the spirit world
To seek forgiveness
Rest in peace dear me.

ME TIME

Do not say I never gave you attention
when I wanted you to know I was busy
busy having an international conversion with me
trying to silence this demons that no longer live under my bed
but in my head

I was busy battling with this thoughts that never give me peace
taking a break from the world
trying to dust myself up
I was busy but screw you
you never seem to understand

I was busy searching for the lost me
deep in the gloomy forest of forlornness
nursing my childhood self
who is always crying for attention
do not say I jilted you
because I was busy collecting my broken pieces
trying to make myself whole again
I was busy in the battlefield
fighting with my raging devils
trying to free myself from emotional detention
yes, I was locked up in a prison of depression
shackled to a web of pain
But look at you
all you do is call me almost twenty times a day
text me insults
Instead of getting better I shrink
I die daily
my pillow is a swamp
I feel neglected
you even said I can't make it?
that has eaten me up
look, what I do is lock up and die
not a physical death but an emotional one
a mental one

I am no more
I just need space
please leave me alone
I am already drowned in a pool of tears
swimming against the tides in a storm of fear
I have lost myself in a forest of sorrow
I can't retrieve my soul
please don't come near me
I am running wild
so mighty bold
just let me be
I will appreciate because I have to do something
learning that what I need is more of me and less world
I have to wipe this tears that never seem to dry
I am finding a perfect mask to hide my face
I need to lock up in the vaults
cry to the lyrical of sad songs
I have to look for a perfect way to end this
until I am done, I will be busy
It is a me time now.

CALL ME A PROSTITUTE

A sex slave
Or rather a chronic drinker
But deep within I know
I am a victim of circumstances
What else could I be
When the woman who gave birth to me
Dumped me in the ruins to die?

Just tell me
What life could I lead ?
when the people who took care of me
regarded me as liquor
so to be abuse left and right
They raped and defiled me every night
Used and threw me into the streets
The whole world turned against me
I chose to seek solace in the bottle

I have seen fingers point at me
My judgement put in black and white
Red on the walls my fate has been written
A big label printed on my face
They call me an addict
But it is life, so I blamelessly take it
What is there to live for
When the canorous bird chirps is a nuisance to me?
I am maimed and the only consolation is the urge to light a cigar
So fast they judge
Even when an anchor to my terrible lifestyle they can't undo
It is not their envisage that anything good can come out of me
But still they gossip of my uselessness
Till the last blink of the sun

Do you think I feel proud
When men dig into my farm day and night

And I have to smile to keep them happy?
Deep down I am shattered
I sell nectar from my flower
Just to pay for my bills
I cry myself to sleep
Proudly they scold me
They take me for a snake in a red rope
Even when the least of my knowledge I plan to attack
I am not an udder
Please stop painting me hate
Non of my actions can be justified
At least my breath can give an account
To my attempt to get a life.

LOST SOUL

I tried searching for true love
In valleys, oceans and mountains above
But lost myself in the dark forest of betrayal
As I tried to be nice by acting loyal
I can't even retrieve my lost soul
From the depths of solitude I cry foul.

www.ingramcontent.com/pod-product-compliance
Ingram Content Group UK Ltd.
Pitfield, Milton Keynes, MK11 3LW, UK
UKHW020237250726
13967UKWH00001B/416